30

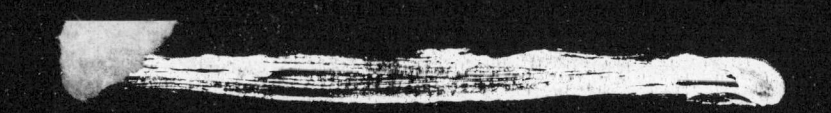

POLLUTION
AND WILDLIFE

© Aladdin Books Ltd 1987

Designed and produced by
Aladdin Books Ltd
70 Old Compton Street
London W1

*First published in
Great Britain in 1987 by*
Franklin Watts
12a Golden Square
London W1

ISBN 0 86313 542 0

The front cover photograph shows a polar bear scavenging on a rubbish tip in Manitoba, Canada. The back cover photograph shows a puffin – the victim of an oil slick.

The author, Michael Bright, is a Senior Producer at the BBC's Natural History Unit, Bristol, UK. He is also the author of several books on Natural History.

The consultant, Noel Simon, worked for the International Union for Conservation of Nature and Natural Resources in Switzerland. He compiled the Mammalia *volume of the* Red Data Book, *the international catalogue of the world's rare and endangered species. He is also the author of many children's books on Natural History.*

Contents

Introduction	4
Pollution worldwide	7
The poisoned fields	8
Insects and pollution	10
Profile: Animals in the food chain	12
Freshwater run-off	14
What a waste	16
Acid rain	18
Profile: Atlantic salmon	20
Oil on the seas	22
The oceanic dustbin	24
Pollution and the individual	26
A cleaner world?	28
Sad facts	30
Useful addresses	31
Index	32

SURVIVAL · SURVIVAL · SURVIVAL

POLLUTION
AND WILDLIFE

Michael Bright

Franklin Watts
London : New York : Toronto : Sydney

Introduction

Over the last fifty years, pollution has become one of the most serious problems facing society. Pollution kills. It chokes rivers, smothers life in the oceans, poisons the air and despoils the land. Pollution is the presence in the environment of large quantities of dangerous chemicals, many created by people, that can harm life and cause long-lasting damage to our planet. Pollution can be obvious, like an oil slick on the surface of the sea, or less obvious, like chemicals sprayed onto fields to kill pests. Pollution is the price the world is paying for rapid agricultural and industrial development – without consideration of its effects on the environment.

Pollution is often the consequence of ignorance, carelessness or attempts to save money when releasing a chemical into the environment. It is not, however, just factories, power stations and farmers who create pollution. We are all responsible, whether driving a car or dropping litter in the street.

Pollution must be controlled, because if the problem is not resolved, then every living thing on this planet could disappear. No organism, no matter how large or how small, can escape the poisonous chemicals of pollution. Pollution has already brought some species of wildlife to the brink of extinction.

Fish all over the world are vulnerable to pollution. A dramatic example occurred after a fire at a chemical plant in Switzerland in November 1986. As a result of the fire, extremely poisonous chemicals were washed into the Rhine River in Europe. Over half a million fish, including 150,000 eels, were wiped out. All life in a 320-kilometre (200-mile) stretch of the river was killed.

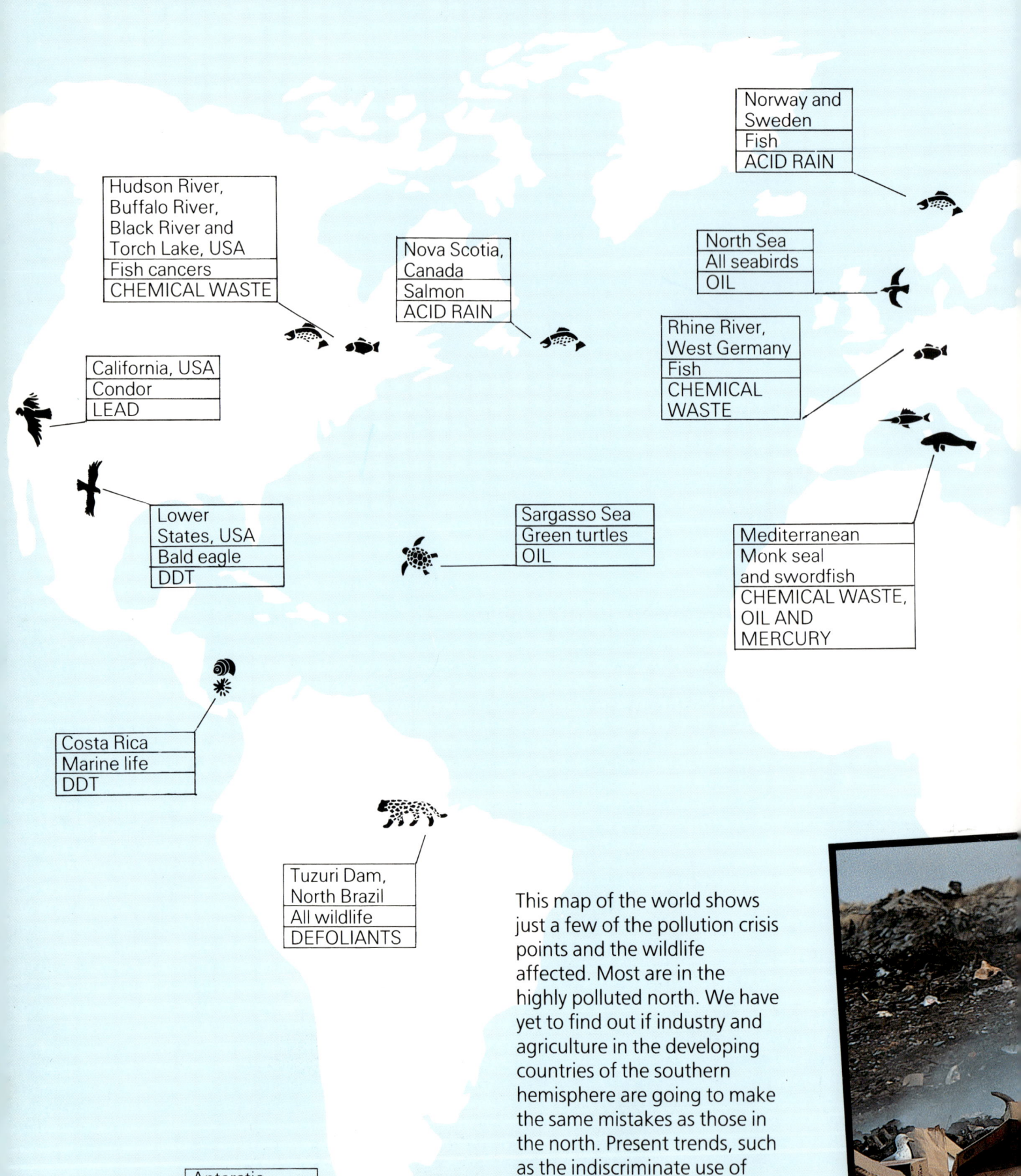

Hudson River, Buffalo River, Black River and Torch Lake, USA
Fish cancers
CHEMICAL WASTE

Nova Scotia, Canada
Salmon
ACID RAIN

Norway and Sweden
Fish
ACID RAIN

North Sea
All seabirds
OIL

Rhine River, West Germany
Fish
CHEMICAL WASTE

California, USA
Condor
LEAD

Lower States, USA
Bald eagle
DDT

Sargasso Sea
Green turtles
OIL

Mediterranean
Monk seal and swordfish
CHEMICAL WASTE, OIL AND MERCURY

Costa Rica
Marine life
DDT

Tuzuri Dam, North Brazil
All wildlife
DEFOLIANTS

Antarctic
Seals and penguins
PESTICIDES AND DDT

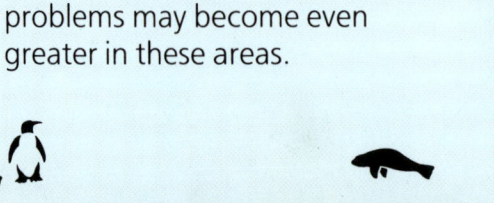

This map of the world shows just a few of the pollution crisis points and the wildlife affected. Most are in the highly polluted north. We have yet to find out if industry and agriculture in the developing countries of the southern hemisphere are going to make the same mistakes as those in the north. Present trends, such as the indiscriminate use of chemicals to kill tropical crop pests, suggest that the problems may become even greater in these areas.

Pollution worldwide

Pollution can be found all over the world. Chemicals created and released in one country will find their way to others. The pollutants are carried by the wind or in ocean currents, and those produced in the agricultural and industrial belts of North America and Europe are finding their way to the remotest parts of the Earth.

Pollution is not new. It was recognised as a problem after the Industrial Revolution, when smoke and soot from factory chimneys killed many living things, including people in the infamous city smogs. Smokeless zones helped solve this problem, but in the 1960s many more frightening forms of pollution began to be recognised. At the UN Conference on the Environment in Stockholm in 1972, all the nations of the world agreed to try to put things right. But today those early dangerous chemical pollutants, and many new ones, are still around in disturbingly large amounts and still presenting a threat to wildlife all over the planet.

▽ In the photograph below, a polar bear digs through a rubbish tip in Manitoba, Canada. Polar bears in the Arctic, hundreds of kilometres from the nearest factory, have been found to have high concentrations of chemical pollutants in their bodies.

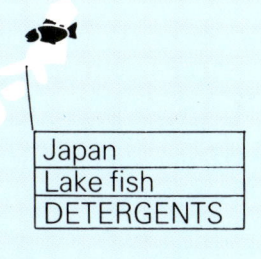

| Japan |
| Lake fish |
| DETERGENTS |

| Papua New Guinea |
| Crocodiles, fish and river turtles |
| CYANIDE FROM GOLD WORKINGS |

The poisoned fields

One of the greatest threats to wildlife is the use of pesticides. Pesticides are poisonous chemicals used, for example, by farmers to kill pests in order to produce healthier, larger crops. However, they not only kill harmful insects but also many other forms of wildlife. The worst offenders are the "persistent" insecticides, such as DDT and dieldrin, that do not break down.

In a food chain, small animals eat the poisons. They, in turn, are eaten by larger animals. The top predators, such as birds of prey, foxes or badgers, gradually accumulate so much poison that they either die or cannot reproduce.

In North America and Europe, DDT and dieldrin have been banned – just in time to save the bald eagle, the sparrow hawk, and the peregrine falcon from extinction. But the chemicals are still to be found in animal tissues, indicating that they are being used illegally. The problem is far from being solved.

The diagram shows how a pesticide might accumulate in a food chain. Seeds coated with pesticide are eaten by pigeons or field mice. They may eat so much of the deadly chemical that they die. Some survive and they carry a small quantity of the poison in their body fat. The seed-eaters are then caught and eaten by a predator, such as a sparrow hawk (photograph right). The hawk may catch several contaminated mice and this gradually builds up a level of pesticide that is either fatal to it, or prevents the bird from breeding.

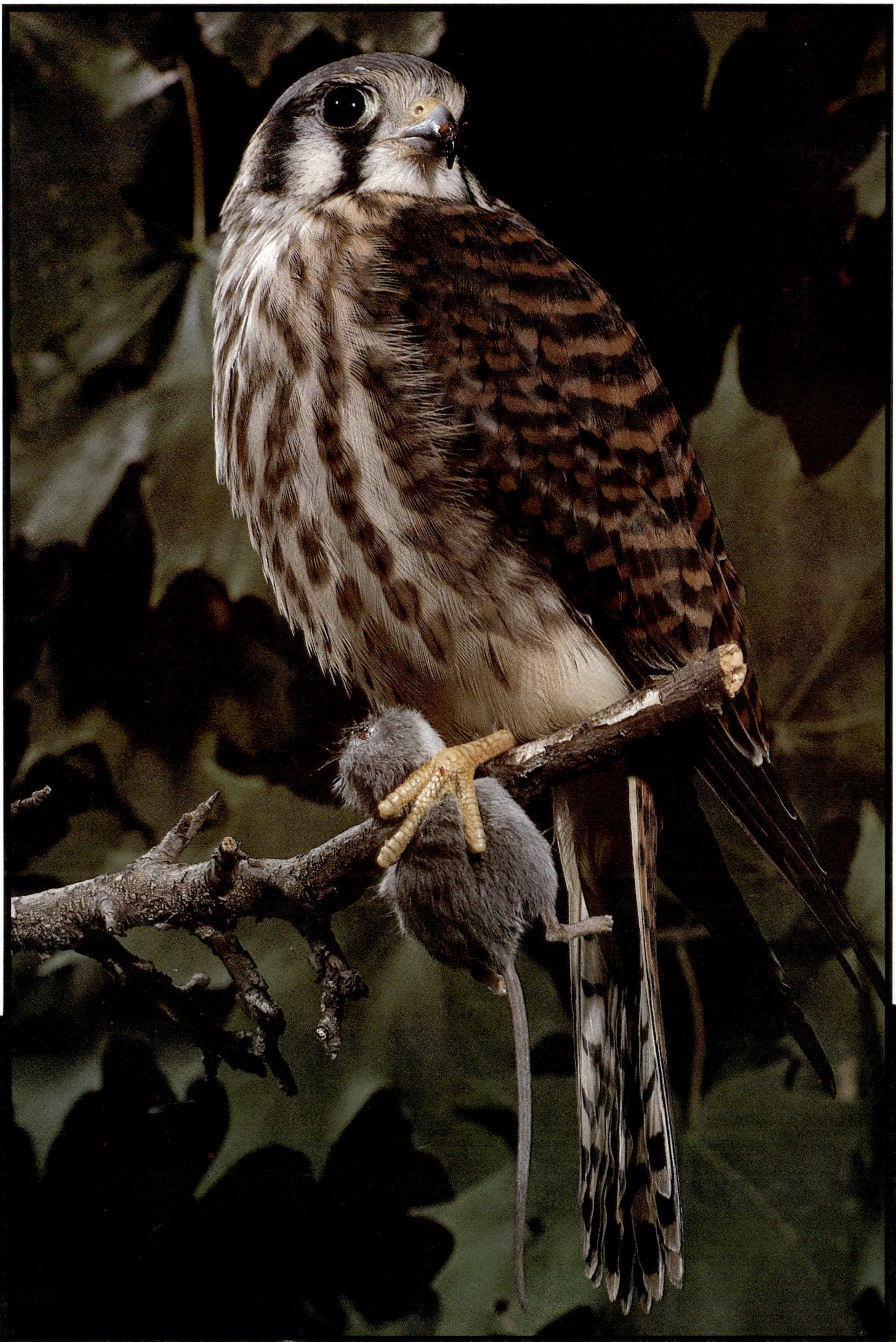

Insects and pollution

Insects are often the first creatures to be hit by pollution but their disappearance is not noticed until other things start to go wrong. Chemicals designed to kill pests also kill harmless, helpful insect life. In Africa, for example, a multi-million dollar chemical-spraying programme attempted to eradicate the tsetse fly – the carrier of "sleeping sickness". Not only did it fail to eliminate the flies, but it also caused the extinction of many species of orchids because pollinating bees were killed. When chemicals are released into the environment we rarely know their long-term effects.

This helicopter is spraying insecticides from the air. Often clouds of the poison miss the target and are blown onto neighbouring land, killing helpful bumblebees and ladybirds (pictures below). In hot, humid conditions the poisons can vaporise and lift off the crop and drift away.

Bumblebee

Ladybird

Adapting to pollution
The peppered moth has adapted to changes in levels of pollution. During the Industrial Revolution, an enormous amount of soot was produced. In order to camouflage itself against predators in the dark, dirty environment, the moth adapted by taking on a darker colouring. Now, with soot, coal fires, and factory wastes under control, some of the moths have gradually changed so that a lighter form also exists.

Not all insects are killed by insecticides. Some have become resistant, while others use the chemicals to their own advantage. In the tropical forests of Brazil, one species of orchid bee actually licks DDT from the walls of village huts and, quite unaffected by the poison, takes it back to the colony where it is used to deter other predatory insects. In the USA the lubber grasshopper has been found to produce a defensive froth containing ingredients normally found in pesticides. In some ways, insects are turning the tables and using pollutants to protect themselves.

SURVIVAL PROFILE...

Animals in the food chain

The consequences of using a pesticide are often not appreciated until long after the event. This is because the poison is "locked up" in a food chain. During the 1940s and 1950s, DDT was widely used to control crop pests. It was more than a decade later that biologists began to recognise the impact of DDT on wildlife.

The peregrine falcon (left) was almost wiped out by DDT. Indeed, across many parts of the intensive cereal-growing regions of North America and northern Europe, the peregrine was totally eradicated. The poison, which had been accumulating in their prey, built up in the birds' body tissues. Some were gradually poisoned. In others the way the body uses calcium was affected. In females this caused eggshells to be abnormally thin so that eggs broke or did not hatch properly. Today, populations are recovering following the banning of DDT.

The American robin's appetite for worms almost led to its extinction. Soil, which had been contaminated with DDT, was eaten by worms, which in turn passed the insecticide on to the robins. The DDT came from an attempt in the USA to destroy the Dutch Elm beetle (below) which carries the fungal spores of Dutch Elm disease. The Dutch Elm beetles were killed and so were a great many other creatures. Now, since DDT is no longer legal, the robin population has increased enormously and is almost back to its normal level.

Dutch Elm beetle

Schaus' swallowtail butterfly

Schaus' swallowtail butterfly was once common in Florida until the mosquitoes sharing the same wetland areas were considered a nuisance and had to be killed. Insecticides were used indiscriminately. Not only were the mosquitoes reduced in numbers but also many other creatures. Schaus' swallowtail was hit so badly that it has been placed on the endangered list.

Freshwater run-off

"Run-off" is the rain or melted snow that flows over the land and ends up in ponds, streams, rivers and lakes. It is usually seriously polluted with the materials farmers put onto fields — pesticides and also fertilisers. In fact, only half the chemical fertiliser applied to a field is taken up by the crop: the rest is washed away.

In polluting freshwater, the fertilisers increase the available plant food, causing a "bloom" of aquatic plant life. This supergrowth of plants, mostly algae that spread like a carpet over the surface of a lake, reduces the amount of oxygen available to aquatic animals and they die. It also impairs the growth of useful oxygen-producing plants below the surface of the lake by preventing the rays of the sun from reaching them.

Polluted run-off is a disturbing problem, and one which is likely to get worse. An increasingly hungry world demands more food and one of the ways to grow it is to use more, not less, fertiliser.

The diagram shows the fate of unused pesticides and fertilisers. (1) The chemicals are applied to the land. (2) Rain washes the chemicals from the soil. (3) Run-off carries them into the lake. (4) Fish concentrate pesticides and quickly build up a lethal level of poison. (5) Otters and herons eat the contaminated fish and accumulate the chemicals. (6) Large amounts of fertilisers cause algae to grow and starve the lake of oxygen.

SURVIVAL PROFILE...

European otter

The otter is a fish-eating aquatic mammal, susceptible to the destruction of its riverbank habitat, disturbance by man, and poisoning by pesticides and industrial wastes washed into rivers.

Despite a ban on DDT and dieldrin, a survey during 1985 revealed that many otters, which may eat a kilogram (2.2 lbs) of contaminated fish a day, are still dying from dieldrin poisoning.

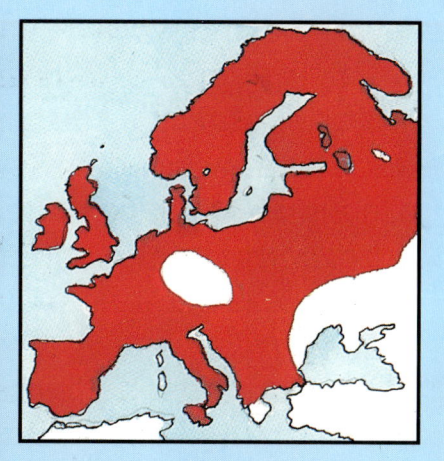

Otters are thinly distributed throughout Europe, indicated by the red areas on the map. In the UK their decline can be accurately dated to 1957, just a year after dieldrin was introduced. Sizeable populations survive today in parts of Scotland, Ireland, and the Atlantic coast of Norway.

What a waste

Rivers have always been used to wash away our waste products to large lakes or to the sea. Some factories and cities discharge untreated waste and sewage in order to save money, and badly-run industrial plants often accidently spill hazardous chemicals into rivers. Poisonous substances entering a river might include mercury from the wood pulp industry and polychlorinated biphenols (PCBs) from plastics manufacture. This polluted water kills many forms of wildlife.

Efforts are being made to monitor and control the problem. In the United States a Clean Water Act was introduced in 1972. Yet today fish in the Great Lakes and in the rivers of the industrial north are still being found with skin and liver cancers caused by pollution. Despite our awareness of the danger of water pollution from industrial wastes, there are few instances of rivers being returned to normal.

Most creatures are killed in seriously polluted water. The diagram shows the variety of water life usually found in unpolluted water (upstream). Some creatures, like those in the polluted area, can live in a soup of toxic chemicals.

Downstream, where the discharge has been diluted, some of the more hardy aquatic animals may return. By collecting specimens from either side of a waste pipe, scientists are able to check for illegal chemical discharges.

◁ A pipe discharges industrial waste into the Blackstone River, Massachusetts, USA.

△ Grey seals in the Baltic Sea have been reduced from 100,000 in 1900 to only 2,000 today. Toxic chemicals have caused malformations in female seals, preventing them from having pups.

Downstream

Bloodworm

Rat-tailed maggot

Tubifex worms

Water slater

Leech

Acid rain

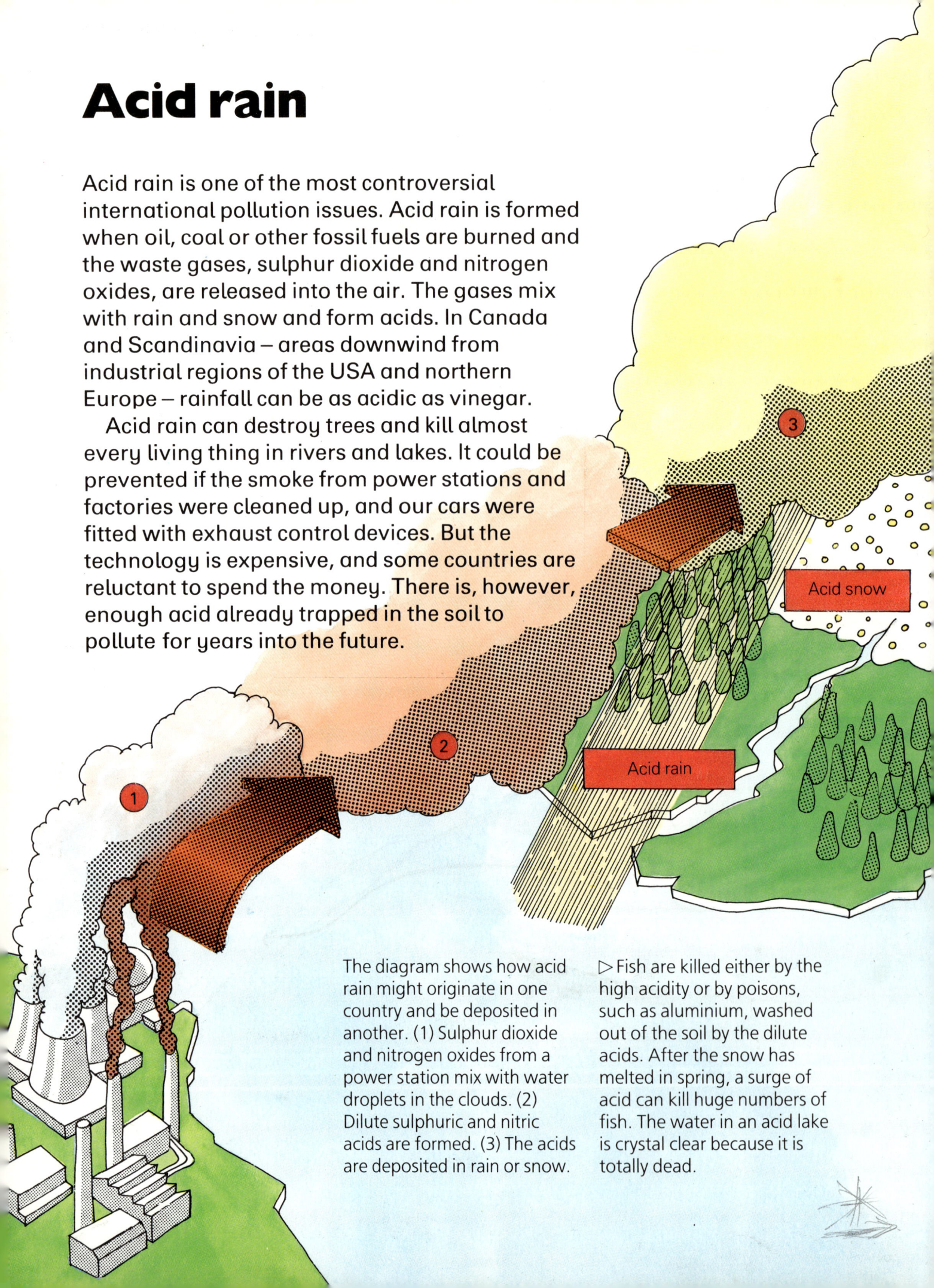

Acid rain is one of the most controversial international pollution issues. Acid rain is formed when oil, coal or other fossil fuels are burned and the waste gases, sulphur dioxide and nitrogen oxides, are released into the air. The gases mix with rain and snow and form acids. In Canada and Scandinavia — areas downwind from industrial regions of the USA and northern Europe — rainfall can be as acidic as vinegar.

Acid rain can destroy trees and kill almost every living thing in rivers and lakes. It could be prevented if the smoke from power stations and factories were cleaned up, and our cars were fitted with exhaust control devices. But the technology is expensive, and some countries are reluctant to spend the money. There is, however, enough acid already trapped in the soil to pollute for years into the future.

The diagram shows how acid rain might originate in one country and be deposited in another. (1) Sulphur dioxide and nitrogen oxides from a power station mix with water droplets in the clouds. (2) Dilute sulphuric and nitric acids are formed. (3) The acids are deposited in rain or snow.

▷ Fish are killed either by the high acidity or by poisons, such as aluminium, washed out of the soil by the dilute acids. After the snow has melted in spring, a surge of acid can kill huge numbers of fish. The water in an acid lake is crystal clear because it is totally dead.

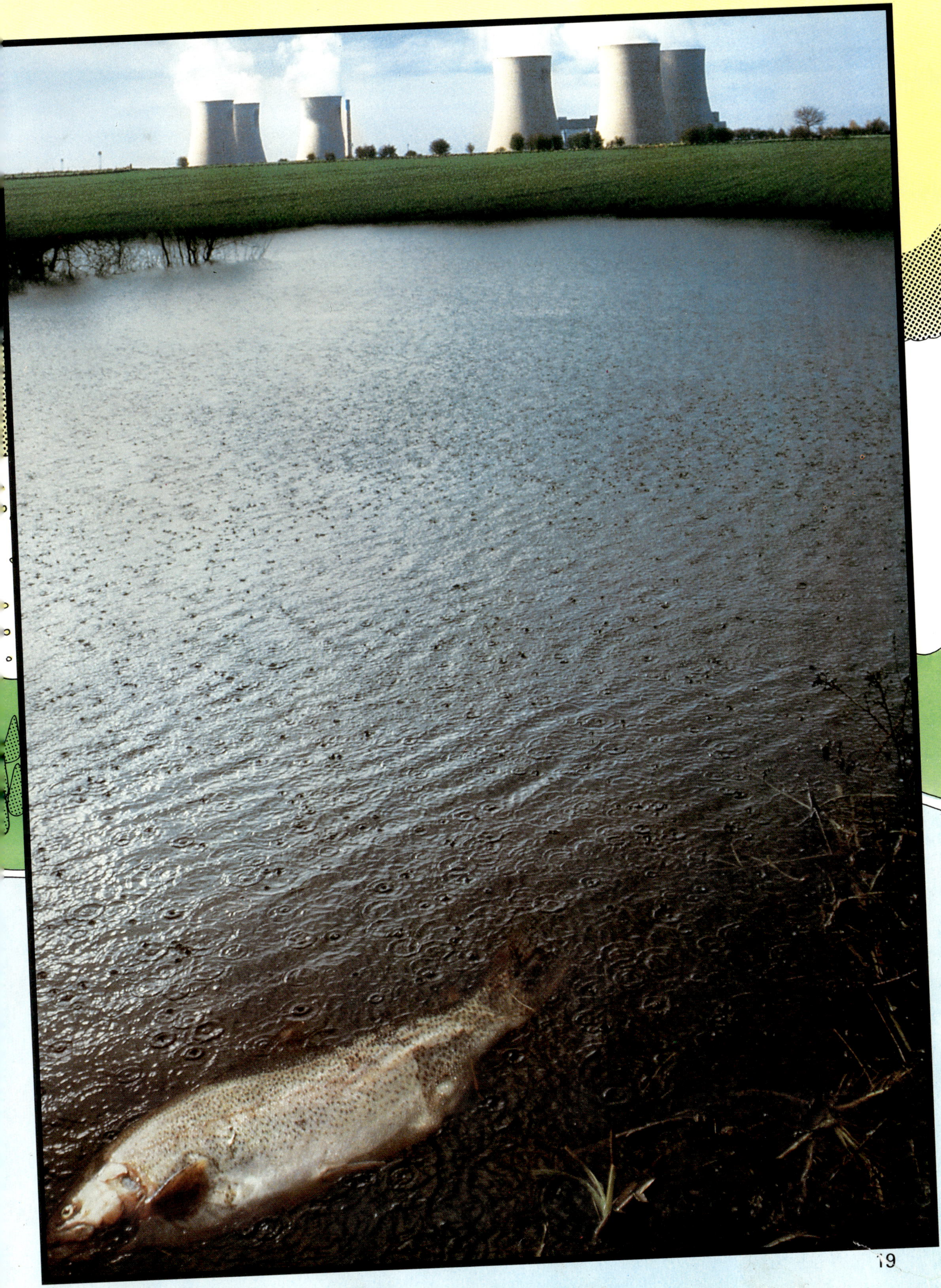

SURVIVAL PROFILE...

Atlantic salmon

Fish are one of the groups of wildlife most seriously affected by pollution. The implications of this are serious – fish are a major food resource. The salmon, for example, is threatened by pollution at each stage of its elaborate life cycle. Some people believe that the wild Atlantic salmon could soon become extinct.

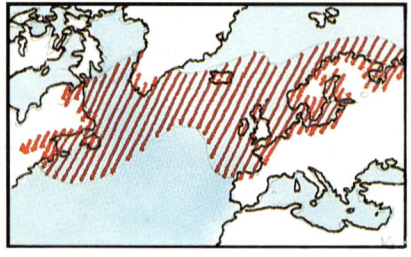

The map shows the distribution of the Atlantic salmon. Fewer salmon will be seen leaping weirs and waterfalls in the rivers flowing into the Atlantic Ocean. The young salmon on its way to the sea and the adult salmon returning to the river must pass through a series of waste pipes from factories and sewage pipes from towns. Poor water quality has destroyed many major salmon runs. Acid rain, falling on the higher reaches of the river, interferes with the adult salmon's ability to find, by smell, its home river. In southern Nova Scotia, Canada, eleven rivers have lost their salmon and several others are threatened. The same is happening in the rest of Canada, Norway, Scotland and Wales.

Development of the salmon

Parr · Fry · Smolt · Alevin · Egg

The eggs are deposited in a gravel pit or "redd" in streams at the head of a major river system. Acid rain prevents the eggs from developing or causes abnormalities to appear in the embryos. When the emerging alevin have used up the food in their yolk-sac, they become fry which feed above the gravel.

Conifer plantations on the banks have no ground-cover so loose top soil clogs the fry "holding pools".

The parr spend two to three years feeding in the rivers, before changing into the silvery smolt which migrate to the sea. They are most susceptible to agricultural run-off. Pesticides, fertilisers, silage effluent, animal excrements from intensively reared stock and battery farms, and animal feed wastes are washed into rivers.

The young salmon spend up to four years at their feeding grounds off southern Greenland in the Atlantic Ocean. The mature fish return to the river of their birth in order to reproduce. After an incredible journey from the sea to the head of the river, a salmon dies (right) before it can spawn. Others, however, reach the redd and scrape a hollow in the gravel in which the eggs and sperm are deposited. Very few of this new generation will return. Acid rain, poisonous chemicals and untreated sewage will take their toll.

Oil on the seas

Oil is found in all the main ocean currents. It is becoming a serious hazard because it does not readily break down, but forms "tar balls" that may drift around the world for years. Tanker spills and oil-well blow-outs hit the headlines because of the dramatic impact on sea shore life, but the greatest contribution to oil pollution is from motorists who change their engine oil and carelessly pour it away. It eventually reaches the sea. Another source is from oil tankers that clean their tanks illegally.

Wildlife, even in the middle of the ocean, is affected. Oil droplets stuck to fish eggs cause abnormalities in the embryo and oil residues poison the nerves of fish larvae. But of all sea creatures, seabirds are most badly hit – they mistake oil slicks for calm water on which they might rest. Their feathers become oiled, and unable to fly, the birds drift with the slick until they die of exposure or starvation.

"Drifting oil clots were observed 40 out of the 57 days it took Ra II to cross the Atlantic."

Thor Heyerdahl, speaking of the voyage of Ra II from Africa to Tropical America

◁ Volunteers and troops clear up France's Brittany coast after the giant oil tanker *Amoco Cadiz* ran aground in March 1978. It was the worst known oil disaster. Another tanker (right) goes down in the Caribbean. Tanker accidents, however, only account for about four per cent of all the oil pollution in the sea.

◁ An oil-covered penguin is cleaned with detergents. This not only removes the sludge, but also natural body oils and so the birds cannot float. They must be looked after for a long time after their rescue before being returned to the sea.

OIL SLICK THREAT

The oceanic dustbin

The oceans, covering seven-tenths of the Earth's surface, have been the traditional dumping places for every kind of waste produced by man. At one time, the oceans were considered so vast that virtually anything poured into the sea would be diluted and any dangerous chemical would be lost for ever. Today, we realise this attitude is totally wrong. The sea is not so large.

However, we still dump untreated sewage, poisonous chemicals, and low-level nuclear waste into the sea. Marine life is under threat. Those creatures living on the bottom of the sea are the first to encounter the poisons. Pollutants are filtered out of the water and concentrate in their flesh. The poisons then build up in the food chain until they are eaten by the ultimate predator – man – often causing food poisoning. Nature, it seems, has an unfailing knack of throwing back our carelessly discarded garbage.

▽ Plastic debris can be a death-trap for wildlife. Gulls scavenge in tideline flotsam and often flip plastic rings, such as the one in the photograph, over their heads and around their necks. Once in place, they work down and strangle the birds.

"The oceans have become the world's sink and the death of the oceans will be the death of us all."

Professor Barry Commoner, speaking to the US Senate Committee on Oceans and the Atmosphere, 1971

This picture shows the extent of the Pacific Ocean – yet even here wildlife cannot escape pollution. A world fleet of 50,000 ships, for example, "disposes" of at least six million tonnes of metal, glass and plastic containers in the world's oceans each day. In the Atlantic, 30 per cent of fish caught have bits of plastic in their gut. But one of the most polluted seas in the world is the Mediterranean. Nearly 85 per cent of all sewage is untreated, and more than two million tonnes of crude oil and 200,000 tonnes of chemical waste, including 100 tonnes of mercury, are poured into it each year. Swordfish and tuna have mercury levels six times higher than in any other sea.

Marine pollution
(1) Plastic nets entangle birds. (2) Oil slicks trap puffins. (3) Baby turtle jaws are gummed up by oil globules. (4) Adult turtles mistake plastic bags for jellyfish and choke to death. (5) Tuna concentrate chemicals in their flesh. (6) Radioactive materials leak and enter the food chain.

Pollution and the individual

Pollution is not just about the dangerous chemicals in factory wastes or the poisons in agricultural pesticides. We, as individuals, also contribute to the suffering of wildlife. Most people keep their homes and gardens neat and tidy, but for some strange reason, they often apply different standards in the countryside or at the seaside. We carelessly discard drinks cans, plastic containers, sweet wrappings, old car tyres and batteries, broken bottles . . . the list is endless, and all can be dangerous for both wild and domestic animals.

A deer foot (below left) caught in a rusty cup. The sharp edges have cut into the flesh making the deer lame. Ducks and other waterfowl pick up the ring-pulls from drinks cans (below), which get caught on the beak, preventing the birds from feeding. In the United States, drinks cans must have non-detachable ring-pulls. Groups of young people in many countries have realised the danger of litter to wildlife and spend their time scouring the countryside and seashore to remove the rubbish that the rest of us have thoughtlessly left behind.

Anglers and hunters contribute to suffering in wildlife. Lead fishing weights and gun shot litter riverbanks where birds eat them and die slowly from lead poisoning. In North America, 75 per cent of mallard ducks die each year from eating lead, whereas only one per cent is shot dead.

The next time you are about to throw something away, whether it be fishing tackle or a drinks can, think of the consequences for wildlife. It is not difficult to put a bottle in the rubbish bin rather than throwing it on the ground. A simple thoughtless act can kill.

SURVIVAL PROFILE...

Field vole

Field vole

Although killed by pollution, predators and habitat destruction, voles maintain their numbers because they are prolific breeders.

Voles worldwide have been hit by various forms of pollution. The discarded bottle in the photograph contains the bones of a field vole which was unable to get out. Many small mammals get trapped in bottles where they drown or starve to death.

The voles of Love Canal, a community of Niagara Falls, in the United States, are dying prematurely from liver damage. The animals have high levels of lindane, a dangerous insecticide and one of the chemicals buried in a waste dump in the suburb.

Voles are in the front line on farms. Grain, with which they supplement their diet of grass, may be coated with pesticides. Any voles not killed immediately are taken by birds of prey and foxes which, in turn, succumb to the accumulated poison.

A cleaner world?

During the past 30 years, the world has gradually realised that pollution has been damaging the environment and killing off wildlife. In Europe and North America several pesticides are now banned (although the United States still exports DDT to developing countries). Factories are reducing the amount of dangerous chemicals released into the air or water. Birds of prey are slowly returning to the countryside and fish are to be found in once-polluted lakes.

There is, however, no room for complacency. Pollution is a problem far from solved and one which is likely to continue. One of the dangers for the future is nuclear wastes — radioactive materials remain active for thousands of years. Moreover, hundreds of new chemicals are created every year, and each one is a potential pollutant. If pollution is not kept in check, not only will wildlife be under threat but also the human race.

Heavily polluted since the 14th century, the Thames in the UK is now a clean river. The photograph on the left shows chemicals being sprayed onto oil in an attempt to clean up pollution in the river. The photograph on the right shows the Thames as it is today — after 30 years of pollution control, salmon and other aquatic life have returned. Attention is now being focused on many other rivers, including those flowing into the Great Lakes of North America and the sewage-filled Ganges in India.

> "The Earth is too important for its future to be left to politicians - or for that matter to the ecologists. It is for all of us."
>
> Sir Peter Scott, one of the founders of the World Wildlife Fund

The dangers of fallout from a nuclear accident, both to wildlife and domestic stock, were made abundantly clear after an explosion at the Chernobyl nuclear power plant in the Soviet Union in 1986. Most of Europe was dusted with radioactive materials that were carried by the wind. Reindeer that had fed on contaminated lichens were slaughtered in Lapland. Cows and sheep throughout Europe continue to be tested. But the real legacy of such an accident will not be known for a long time in the future.

Sad facts

Brazil
The huge petrochemical and industrial complex of Cubatao, near Sao Paulo, is known as the Valley of Death. Each day, 1,000 tonnes of noxious gases are released from 22 petrochemical and steel plants. The four rivers flowing through the area are dead, trees and soil are lifeless, and there are no birds.

France
The grey partridge has all but disappeared in western Europe because the insects on which the chicks feed have been killed by insecticides. Many creatures die when a food chain is interrupted by the removal of a link.

Iran and Iraq
Dugongs, or sea cows, living along the shores of the Gulf of Arabia, are threatened with local extinction because of war damage to oil installations.

Japan
Many of Japan's lakes and inland seas have been turning red or green, following "blooms" of algae that feed on the phosphates from detergents.

The Netherlands
Off the Dutch coast, 40 per cent of the flounders, dabs and plaice have been found with cancerous skin tumours caused by industrial wastes.

Papua New Guinea
Huge quantities of cyanide, used in the processing of gold and copper, have been spilling into the Ok Tedi River, one of the main rivers in the country. In one major incident the river was blocked by dead crocodiles, turtles and fish.

Poland
Wildlife in the highly industrial region around Katowice, near Cracow has little chance of survival when 7 tonnes of cadmium, 170 tonnes of lead and 470 tonnes of zinc dust are ejected from factory chimneys each year.

Sweden
Before restrictions on the use of pesticides, an estimated 10,000 starlings died when they ate insects coated with DDT. The yellowhammer became locally extinct in the agricultural south.

White-tailed sea eagles were hit badly after eating fish containing high levels of DDT, PCBs and mercury in the Baltic Sea. A recovery programme, involving the placing of uncontaminated meat baits, is only now beginning to show signs of success.

United Kingdom
In the UK, 4,000 mute swans out of the total population of 18,000 are killed each year after eating tiny lead fishing weights discarded by anglers.

Incidents of farm waste pollution, including spills and leaks of farm wastes, and farmyard run-off, rose by 25 per cent in England and Wales during 1985.

United States
The California condor has become extinct in the wild. The birds were poisoned by the lead in deer and other carrion shot by hunters.

Tern chicks on Great Gull Island, New York, are appearing with serious body deformities and loss of feathers. The cause is thought to be a build-up of dangerous chemicals in fish, which is their primary food.

In Michigan, in 1980, wastes from automobile factories, steel mills, oil refineries and chemical plants were found in an abandoned chemical dump. Ponds nearby contained a stew of cyanide, acids, PCBs and pesticides. The clean-up, including the removal and reburial of 120,000 tonnes of waste and contaminated soil, is still going on, while fish in nearby rivers show signs of skin and liver cancers. There are thousands of similar sites in the USA.

Over 80 per cent of the fish in the Duwamish River in Washington, the Buffalo and Hudson Rivers in New York State, the Black River in Ohio, and Torch Lake, Michigan, have skin or liver cancers.

USSR

Life in and around the 25 million year old Lake Baikal – the deepest lake in the world – has been under threat from chemical effluents. Of particular concern is the Baikal seal. It is one of the few freshwater seals in the world and is the top predator in a food chain that starts with a freshwater "shrimp" that is killed by the noxious chemicals.

West Germany

Automobile fumes are being blamed for the destruction of forests and the accompanying loss of wildlife. It is thought that all the conifers in the Black Forest will be dead by the end of the century.

Zimbabwe

The spraying of persistent pesticides for locust, mosquito and tsetse fly control is affecting other wildlife. Fish eagles are showing signs of eggshell thinning.

Useful addresses

Friends of the Earth
377 City Road, London
EC1V 1NA

Friends of the Earth (Scotland)
53 George IV Bridge,
Edinburgh EH1 1EJ

Greenpeace
36 Graham Street,
London N1 8LL

National Society for Clean Air
136 North Street, Brighton,
East Sussex BN1 1RG

The Royal Society for Nature Conservation
The Green, Nettleham, Lincoln
LN2 2NR

The Royal Society for the Protection of Birds and The Young Ornithologists' Club
The Lodge, Sandy,
Bedfordshire SG19 2DL

World Wildlife Fund
11-13 Ockford Road,
Godalming, Surrey GU7 1QU

Australia and New Zealand
The RSPCA, Wildlife and National Parks' services provide information in all capitals and regional centres and can be contacted through the telephone directory.

A gannet killed by a carelessly discarded fishing net.

Index

A acid rain, 6, 18, 20, 21
agriculture, 4, 6, 7, 8, 10, 12, 14, 21, 26
air, 4, 18, 28
animals, 8, 9, 12, 13, 14, 15, 27

B badgers, 8
birds, 6, 8, 12, 14, 24, 25, 26, 27, 28, 30, 31

C chemicals, 4, 5, 6, 7, 8, 10, 11, 14, 15, 16, 17, 21, 24, 25, 27, 28, 30, 31
condor, 6, 30
crocodiles, 7, 30

D DDT, 6, 8, 11, 12, 13, 15, 28, 30
defoliants, 6
detergents, 6, 7, 30
dieldrin, 8, 15, 27, 28

E environment, 4, 5, 7, 10, 11, 28
extinction, 5, 8, 10, 12, 15, 18, 20, 30

F fertilisers, 14, 21
field mice, 8
field vole, 27
fish, 5, 6, 7, 14, 15, 16, 18, 19, 20, 21, 22, 25, 28, 30
food chains, 5, 8, 9, 12, 13, 24, 25, 30, 31
forests, 31
foxes, 8

H heron, 14

I Industrial Revolution, 7
industrial waste, 4, 6, 7, 15, 16, 17, 28, 30
insecticides, *see* pesticides
insects, 8, 10, 11, 13, 30

L lakes, 6, 7, 14, 16, 18, 28, 30, 31
litter, 5, 26, 27

N nuclear waste, 24, 28

O oceans, 4, 7, 22, 24-25
oil industry, 18, 22, 25
oil slicks, 4, 6, 22, 23, 28
otters, 14, 15
oxygen, 14

P PCBs, 16, 30
penguins, 6, 23
peregrine falcon, 8, 12
pesticides, 4, 6, 8, 9, 10, 11, 12, 13, 14, 15, 21, 26, 27, 30, 31
plants, 10, 14
poisons, 6, 7, 14, 15, 16, 18, 21, 24, 25, 27, 30, 31
polar bears, 7
ponds, 14, 30
power stations, 5, 18
puffins, 25

R radioactivity, 25, 28, 29
rivers, 4, 6, 7, 14, 15, 16, 17, 18, 20, 21, 28, 30
run-off, 14, 15

S seabirds, 6, 22, 23, 24, 26, 30
seals, 6, 17, 31
seas, 16, 22, 23, 24, 25, 30
sewage, 16, 20, 21, 25, 28
soil, 13, 14, 18, 30
streams, 14

T trees, 18, 21, 30, 31
turtles, 6, 7, 25, 30

W waste gases, 18, 30
waste products, 16, 17, 20, 21, 24, 28, 30
water, 14, 16, 18, 20, 28

Photographic Credits:
Cover and pages 7 and 12: Bruce Colman; pages 4-5 and 26: Robert Harding; pages 9 and 24: Oxford Scientific Films; pages 10 and 20: Picturepoint; page 11: Mark Collins; pages 11, 13, 16-17, 17, 21, 23, 26, 27 and back cover: Ardea; page 15: Zefa; page 19: Sandy Porter/Sunday Times; page 22: Camera Press; page 28: Spectrum; page 29: Associated Press.